Victoria Rey

Money Spells

© All rights reserved. No part of this book may be reproduced in text or images by any means, without written permission.

© Calli Casa Editorial 2013
© Yhacar Trust, 2024

General Supervision: Bernabé Pérez.
www.2GoodLuck.com
Calli Casa Editorial
Lake Elsinore, CA 92530

INTRODUCTION

Have you ever felt like money is a mystical force, flowing freely to some and stubbornly out of reach for others?

The truth is, there's more to financial abundance than just hard work and a good education. Our beliefs, habits, and even the energy we project can play a significant role in attracting or repelling prosperity.

This book is your guide to unlocking the magic within yourself and the universe to cultivate financial security and abundance. We'll delve into the world of money spells, a practice that combines intention-setting, symbolic actions, and the power of positive thinking to shift your financial reality.

HERE'S WHAT YOU'LL FIND INSIDE:

- The fundamental principles of money magic – intention, visualization, gratitude, and action.
- 31 daily money spells – a ritual for each day of the month to solidify your financial goals and create positive habits.
- Techniques for cultivating an abundance mindset – shifting your perspective from scarcity to limitless possibility.
- Daydream exercises to tap into the power of the Universe and open yourself up to receiving financial abundance.
- Practical financial planning tips – because magic works best alongside real-world strategies.

Here's a list of spells:

PERSONAL FINANCE SPELLS

Wealth Attraction Spell
Debt Reduction Spell
Savings Growth Spell
Emergency Fund Spell
Financial Protection Spell
Prosperity Jar Spell
Money Manifestation Spell
Employment Success Spell
Investment Luck Spell
Unexpected Windfall Spell
Good Credit Spell

BUSINESS FINANCE SPELLS

Business Success Spell
Client Attraction Spell
Sales Boost Spell
Profit Increase Spell
Partnership Harmony Spell
Startup Funding Spell
Market Expansion Spell
Innovation and Creativity Spell
Business Protection Spell
Employee Loyalty Spell
Debt Collection Spell

CASINO AND GAMBLING SPELLS

Lucky Hand Spell
Winning Streak Spell
Slot Machine Luck Spell
Poker Fortune Spell
Roulette Success Spell
Lottery Winning Spell
Betting Wisdom Spell
Safe Gambling Spell
Jackpot Attraction Spell

WHETHER YOU'RE LOOKING TO:

- Pay off debt and achieve financial freedom
- Manifest a raise or dream job
- Attract unexpected windfalls
- Develop a healthy relationship with money

This book will empower you to take charge of your finances and create a life overflowing with abundance.

Are you ready to unlock the magic of money? **Let's begin!**

WEALTH ATTRACTION SPELL

PURPOSE: TO ATTRACT WEALTH AND PROSPERITY INTO YOUR LIFE.

MATERIALS NEEDED:

1 green candle

Money-drawing oil (or a mix of cinnamon, basil, and patchouli essential oils)

Gold glitter (optional)

Basil and cinnamon herbs

Patchouli incense

PREPARATION:

Choose a quiet and comfortable place where you won't be disturbed.

Gather all your materials and place them on a clean surface.

ANOINT THE CANDLE:

Take the green candle and hold it in your hands. Close your eyes and visualize yourself surrounded by wealth and prosperity.

Anoint the candle with the money-drawing oil. Start from the middle of the candle, moving upward to the wick, and then from the middle down to the base. As you do this, focus on your intention to attract wealth.

(Optional) Sprinkle a little gold glitter on the candle to enhance the spell's power.

DRESS THE CANDLE:

Roll the anointed candle in the basil and cinnamon herbs, ensuring they stick to the oil. These herbs are known for their wealth-attracting properties.

SET UP THE SPACE:

Place the dressed candle in a candle holder and set it in front of you.

Light the patchouli incense and let the fragrant smoke fill the air. Patchouli is associated with abundance and financial success.

CASTING THE SPELL:

Light the green candle and say the following words:

By the light of this flame, wealth I seek,

Prosperity and abundance into my life now leak.

With basil, cinnamon, and patchouli's might,

Attracting wealth and fortune tonight.

So mote it be.

Visualize yourself receiving money from various sources. See yourself paying off debts, saving money, and enjoying financial freedom.

MEDITATION:

Sit quietly for a few minutes, focusing on the flame and continuing to visualize wealth flowing into your life.

Feel gratitude for the abundance that is coming your way.

CLOSING THE SPELL:

Let the candle burn completely. If you must leave it unattended, extinguish it and relight it when you can continue to focus on your intention.

Once the candle has burned out, bury any remaining wax and herbs in the earth to ground the spell and make it manifest.

Remember to believe in the power of your intention and the spell you cast. Your mindset and positive energy play a crucial role in manifesting wealth and prosperity.

DEBT REDUCTION SPELL

PURPOSE: TO HELP REDUCE AND ELIMINATE DEBT.

MATERIALS NEEDED:

1 black candle

Debt-banishing oil (a mix of rosemary, lemon, and clove essential oils)

Salt

Bay leaves

Frankincense incense

PREPARATION:

Find a quiet and undisturbed place to perform the spell.

Gather all your materials and place them on a clean surface.

ANOINT THE CANDLE:

Hold the black candle in your hands and close your eyes. Visualize yourself free from debt and financial burdens.

Anoint the candle with the debt-banishing oil. Start from the middle of the candle, moving upward to the wick, and then from the middle down to the base. As you do this, focus on your intention to eliminate debt.

DRESS THE CANDLE:

Roll the anointed candle in the salt. Salt is known for its purifying and banishing properties.

Place a few bay leaves around the base of the candle. Bay leaves are associated with protection and success in financial matters.

SET UP THE SPACE:

Place the dressed candle in a candle holder and set it in front of you.

Light the frankincense incense to purify the space and enhance your focus.

CASTING THE SPELL:

Light the black candle and say the following words:

By this flame, my debts take flight,

Disappearing into the night.

With rosemary, lemon, and clove's power,

My financial freedom now does flower.

So mote it be.

Visualize your debts diminishing and your financial burdens lifting. See yourself paying off debts and feeling relieved and free.

MEDITATION:

Sit quietly for a few minutes, focusing on the flame and continuing to visualize the elimination of your debts.

Feel the weight of your financial burdens lifting and experience the sense of freedom and relief.

CLOSING THE SPELL:

Let the candle burn completely. If you must leave it unattended, extinguish it and relight it when you can continue to focus on your intention.

Once the candle has burned out, bury any remaining wax, salt, and bay leaves in the earth to ground the spell and solidify the banishing of your debts.

By believing in your power to change your financial situation, you can effectively manifest debt reduction through this spell.

SAVINGS GROWTH SPELL

PURPOSE: TO HELP INCREASE AND GROW YOUR SAVINGS.

MATERIALS NEEDED:

1 yellow candle

Prosperity oil (a mix of orange, bergamot, and ginger essential oils)

Chamomile and clover herbs

Cinnamon incense

PREPARATION:

Find a quiet and undisturbed place to perform the spell.

Gather all your materials and place them on a clean surface.

ANOINT THE CANDLE:

Hold the yellow candle in your hands and close your eyes. Visualize your savings account growing and your financial security increasing.

Anoint the candle with the prosperity oil. Start from the middle of the candle, moving upward to the wick, and then from the middle down to the base. As you do this, focus on your intention to grow your savings.

DRESS THE CANDLE:

Roll the anointed candle in the chamomile and clover herbs. These herbs are associated with prosperity and financial growth.

SET UP THE SPACE:

Place the dressed candle in a candle holder and set it in front of you.

Light the cinnamon incense to attract prosperity and enhance your focus.

CASTING THE SPELL:

Light the yellow candle and say the following words:

> By this flame, my savings grow,
>
> Prosperity and abundance flow.
>
> With orange, bergamot, and ginger's might,
>
> My financial security takes flight.
>
> So mote it be.

Visualize your savings account growing, see deposits being made, and feel the security of having a healthy savings balance.

MEDITATION:

Sit quietly for a few minutes, focusing on the flame and continuing to visualize the growth of your savings.

Feel gratitude for the financial security and prosperity coming your way.

CLOSING THE SPELL:

Let the candle burn completely. If you must leave it unattended, extinguish it and relight it when you can continue to focus on your intention.

Once the candle has burned out, bury any remaining wax and herbs in the earth to ground the spell and make it manifest.

Believing in your ability to grow your savings will help you manifest financial security and abundance.

EMERGENCY FUND SPELL

PURPOSE: TO HELP CREATE AND MAINTAIN AN EMERGENCY FUND FOR UNEXPECTED EXPENSES.

MATERIALS NEEDED:

1 white candle

Stability oil (a mix of lavender, cedarwood, and sandalwood essential oils)

Mint and rosemary herbs

Sage incense

PREPARATION:

Find a quiet and undisturbed place to perform the spell.

Gather all your materials and place them on a clean surface.

ANOINT THE CANDLE:

Hold the white candle in your hands and close your eyes. Visualize having a secure emergency fund that covers unexpected expenses.

Anoint the candle with the stability oil. Start from the middle of the candle, moving upward to the wick, and then from the middle down to the base. As you do this, focus on your intention to build and maintain an emergency fund.

DRESS THE CANDLE:

Roll the anointed candle in the mint and rosemary herbs. These herbs are known for their protective and stabilizing properties.

SET UP THE SPACE:

Place the dressed candle in a candle holder and set it in front of you.

Light the sage incense to cleanse the space and enhance your focus.

CASTING THE SPELL:

Light the white candle and say the following words:

> By this flame, my fund takes hold,
> Stability and security, my goal bold.
> With lavender, cedarwood, and sandalwood's grace,
> My emergency fund finds its place.
> So mote it be.

Visualize your emergency fund growing and feel the peace of mind that comes with financial security.

MEDITATION:

Sit quietly for a few minutes, focusing on the flame and continuing to visualize the growth and maintenance of your emergency fund.

Feel gratitude for the financial security and peace of mind that your emergency fund provides.

CLOSING THE SPELL:

Let the candle burn completely. If you must leave it unattended, extinguish it and relight it when you can continue to focus on your intention.

Once the candle has burned out, bury any remaining wax and herbs in the earth to ground the spell and make it manifest.

FINANCIAL PROTECTION SPELL

PURPOSE: TO PROTECT YOUR FINANCES FROM LOSS AND UNFORESEEN EXPENSES.

MATERIALS NEEDED:

1 blue candle

Protection oil (a mix of eucalyptus, frankincense, and myrrh essential oils)

Bay leaf and sage herbs

Dragon's blood incense

PREPARATION:

Find a quiet and undisturbed place to perform the spell.

Gather all your materials and place them on a clean surface.

ANOINT THE CANDLE:

Hold the blue candle in your hands and close your eyes. Visualize your finances being shielded from harm and unexpected expenses.

Anoint the candle with the protection oil. Start from the middle of the candle, moving upward to the wick, and then from the middle down to the base. As you do this, focus on your intention to protect your finances.

DRESS THE CANDLE:

Roll the anointed candle in the bay leaf and sage herbs. These herbs are associated with protection and purification.

SET UP THE SPACE:

Place the dressed candle in a candle holder and set it in front of you.

Light the dragon's blood incense to enhance the protective energy of the spell.

CASTING THE SPELL:

Light the blue candle and say the following words:

By this flame, protection I seek,

Shield my finances, strong and sleek.

With eucalyptus, frankincense, and myrrh's might,

Guard my wealth both day and night.

So mote it be.

Visualize a protective barrier around your finances, keeping them safe from harm and unforeseen expenses.

MEDITATION:

Sit quietly for a few minutes, focusing on the flame and continuing to visualize the protection of your finances.

Feel a sense of security and assurance that your finances are protected.

CLOSING THE SPELL:

Let the candle burn completely. If you must leave it unattended, extinguish it and relight it when you can continue to focus on your intention.

Once the candle has burned out, bury any remaining wax and herbs in the earth to ground the spell and solidify the protection of your finances.

PROSPERITY JAR SPELL
PURPOSE: TO CREATE A PROSPERITY JAR THAT ATTRACTS ONGOING WEALTH AND ABUNDANCE.

MATERIALS NEEDED:

1 green candle

Prosperity oil (a mix of cinnamon, clove, and nutmeg essential oils)

A small jar with a lid

Coins, basil, and bay leaves

Patchouli incense

PREPARATION:

Find a quiet and undisturbed place to perform the spell.

Gather all your materials and place them on a clean surface.

ANOINT THE CANDLE:

Hold the green candle in your hands and close your eyes. Visualize ongoing wealth and abundance flowing into your life.

Anoint the candle with the prosperity oil. Start from the middle of the candle, moving upward to the wick, and then from the middle down to the base. As you do this, focus on your intention to attract ongoing wealth.

PREPARE THE JAR:

Fill the jar with coins, basil, and bay leaves. These items symbolize wealth, prosperity, and protection.

Seal the jar with its lid.

SET UP THE SPACE:

Place the dressed candle in a candle holder and set it in front of you.

Light the patchouli incense to attract prosperity and enhance your focus.

CASTING THE SPELL:

Light the green candle and say the following words:

> *By this flame, prosperity I jar,*
> *Wealth and abundance, never far.*
> *With cinnamon, clove, and nutmeg's blend,*
> *My financial fortunes, now ascend.*
> *So mote it be.*

Visualize the jar filling with wealth and abundance, attracting prosperity into your life continuously.

MEDITATION:

Sit quietly for a few minutes, focusing on the flame and continuing to visualize ongoing wealth and abundance.

Feel gratitude for the continuous flow of prosperity into your life.

CLOSING THE SPELL:

Let the candle burn completely. If you must leave it unattended, extinguish it and relight it when you can continue to focus on your intention.

Once the candle has burned out, place the jar in a safe place where it won't be disturbed. Shake it occasionally to activate the spell and attract more prosperity.

MONEY MANIFESTATION SPELL

PURPOSE: TO MANIFEST MONEY QUICKLY AND EFFICIENTLY INTO YOUR LIFE.

MATERIALS NEEDED:

1 gold candle

Manifestation oil (a mix of bergamot, jasmine, and orange essential oils)

Ginger and nutmeg herbs

Jasmine incense

PREPARATION:

Find a quiet and undisturbed place to perform the spell.

Gather all your materials and place them on a clean surface.

ANOINT THE CANDLE:

Hold the gold candle in your hands and close your eyes. Visualize money flowing into your life quickly and effortlessly.

Anoint the candle with the manifestation oil. Start from the middle of the candle, moving upward to the wick, and then from the middle down to the base. As you do this, focus on your intention to manifest money.

DRESS THE CANDLE:

Roll the anointed candle in the ginger and nutmeg herbs. These herbs are known for their ability to attract money and enhance manifestation.

SET UP THE SPACE:

Place the dressed candle in a candle holder and set it in front of you.

Light the jasmine incense to attract prosperity and enhance your focus.

CASTING THE SPELL:

Light the gold candle and say the following words:

> By this flame, money I draw,
> Manifesting wealth with fast flaw.
> With bergamot, jasmine, and orange's might,
> Financial abundance in my sight.
> So mote it be.

Visualize money flowing into your life, see yourself receiving unexpected financial blessings, and feel the joy of financial freedom.

MEDITATION:

Sit quietly for a few minutes, focusing on the flame and continuing to visualize the manifestation of money.

Feel gratitude for the financial abundance that is manifesting in your life.

CLOSING THE SPELL:

Let the candle burn completely. If you must leave it unattended, extinguish it and relight it when you can continue to focus on your intention.

Once the candle has burned out, bury any remaining wax and herbs in the earth to ground the spell and make it manifest.

EMPLOYMENT SUCCESS SPELL

PURPOSE: TO HELP SECURE A JOB OR ACHIEVE SUCCESS IN YOUR CURRENT EMPLOYMENT.

MATERIALS NEEDED:

1 yellow candle

Success oil (a mix of rosemary, bergamot, and cedarwood essential oils)

Sunflower petals and dill herbs

Rosemary incense

PREPARATION:

Find a quiet and undisturbed place to perform the spell.

Gather all your materials and place them on a clean surface.

ANOINT THE CANDLE:

Hold the yellow candle in your hands and close your eyes. Visualize yourself securing the job you desire or achieving success in your current employment.

Anoint the candle with the success oil. Start from the middle of the candle, moving upward to the wick, and then from the middle down to the base. As you do this, focus on your intention to succeed in employment.

DRESS THE CANDLE:

Roll the anointed candle in the sunflower petals and dill herbs. These herbs are known for their ability to attract success and good fortune.

SET UP THE SPACE:

Place the dressed candle in a candle holder and set it in front of you.

Light the rosemary incense to enhance your focus and attract success.

CASTING THE SPELL:

Light the yellow candle and say the following words:

By this flame, success I seek,

Employment goals, now I speak.

With rosemary, bergamot, and cedarwood's aid,

My career path, now well laid.

So mote it be.

Visualize yourself excelling in your job, receiving positive feedback, and achieving your career goals.

MEDITATION:

Sit quietly for a few minutes, focusing on the flame and continuing to visualize success in your employment.

Feel confidence and determination in your career path.

CLOSING THE SPELL:

Let the candle burn completely. If you must leave it unattended, extinguish it and relight it when you can continue to focus on your intention.

Once the candle has burned out, bury any remaining wax and herbs in the earth to ground the spell and solidify your success.

INVESTMENT LUCK SPELL

PURPOSE: TO ATTRACT LUCK AND SUCCESS IN YOUR INVESTMENTS.

MATERIALS NEEDED:

1 green candle

Luck oil (a mix of clover, basil, and cinnamon essential oils)

Mint and basil herbs

Lavender incense

PREPARATION:

Find a quiet and undisturbed place to perform the spell.

Gather all your materials and place them on a clean surface.

ANOINT THE CANDLE:

Hold the green candle in your hands and close your eyes. Visualize your investments growing and yielding positive returns.

Anoint the candle with the luck oil. Start from the middle of the candle, moving upward to the wick, and then from the middle down to the base. As you do this, focus on your intention to attract luck in your investments.

DRESS THE CANDLE:

Roll the anointed candle in the mint and basil herbs. These herbs are known for their ability to attract luck and prosperity.

SET UP THE SPACE:

Place the dressed candle in a candle holder and set it in front of you.

Light the lavender incense to enhance your focus and attract good fortune.

CASTING THE SPELL:

Light the green candle and say the following words:

By this flame, luck I claim,

Investments grow, returns untamed.

With clover, basil, and cinnamon's might,

Financial success, now in sight.

So mote it be.

Visualize your investments thriving and yielding positive returns. See yourself making wise financial decisions.

MEDITATION:

Sit quietly for a few minutes, focusing on the flame and continuing to visualize success and luck in your investments.

Feel confidence and assurance in your investment choices.

CLOSING THE SPELL:

Let the candle burn completely. If you must leave it unattended, extinguish it and relight it when you can continue to focus on your intention.

Once the candle has burned out, bury any remaining wax and herbs in the earth to ground the spell and make it manifest.

UNEXPECTED WINDFALL SPELL

PURPOSE: TO ATTRACT UNEXPECTED MONEY OR FINANCIAL BLESSINGS.

MATERIALS NEEDED:

1 gold candle

Windfall oil (a mix of frankincense, myrrh, and sandalwood essential oils)

Bay leaf and cinnamon herbs

Frankincense incense

PREPARATION:

Find a quiet and undisturbed place to perform the spell.

Gather all your materials and place them on a clean surface.

ANOINT THE CANDLE:

Hold the gold candle in your hands and close your eyes. Visualize unexpected money or financial blessings coming into your life.

Anoint the candle with the windfall oil. Start from the middle of the candle, moving upward to the wick, and then from the middle down to the base. As you do this, focus on your intention to attract unexpected money.

DRESS THE CANDLE:

Roll the anointed candle in the bay leaf and cinnamon herbs. These herbs are associated with prosperity and good fortune.

SET UP THE SPACE:

Place the dressed candle in a candle holder and set it in front of you.

Light the frankincense incense to enhance your focus and attract financial blessings.

CASTING THE SPELL:

Light the gold candle and say the following words:

By this flame, blessings I call,

Unexpected money, into my life fall.

With frankincense, myrrh, and sandalwood's light,

Financial abundance, now in sight.

So mote it be.

Visualize unexpected money or financial blessings coming into your life. See yourself receiving a surprise windfall.

MEDITATION:

Sit quietly for a few minutes, focusing on the flame and continuing to visualize unexpected financial blessings.

Feel gratitude for the unexpected money and blessings that are coming your way.

CLOSING THE SPELL:

Let the candle burn completely. If you must leave it unattended, extinguish it and relight it when you can continue to focus on your intention.

Once the candle has burned out, bury any remaining wax and herbs in the earth to ground the spell and make it manifest.

GOOD CREDIT SPELL

PURPOSE: TO IMPROVE AND MAINTAIN A GOOD CREDIT SCORE.

MATERIALS NEEDED:

1 blue candle

Credit improvement oil (a mix of lemon, rosemary, and eucalyptus essential oils)

Basil and clove herbs

Sandalwood incense

PREPARATION:

Find a quiet and undisturbed place to perform the spell.

Gather all your materials and place them on a clean surface.

ANOINT THE CANDLE:

Hold the blue candle in your hands and close your eyes. Visualize your credit score improving and your credit history being positive.

Anoint the candle with the credit improvement oil. Start from the middle of the candle, moving upward to the wick, and then from the middle down to the base. As you do this, focus on your intention to improve your credit score.

DRESS THE CANDLE:

Roll the anointed candle in the basil and clove herbs. These herbs are known for their ability to attract prosperity and improve financial situations.

SET UP THE SPACE:

Place the dressed candle in a candle holder and set it in front of you.

Light the sandalwood incense to enhance your focus and attract positive financial energy.

CASTING THE SPELL:

Light the blue candle and say the following words:

By this flame, my credit soars,
Financial health forevermore.
With lemon, rosemary, and eucalyptus pure,
My credit score, strong and sure.
So mote it be.

Visualize your credit score improving and your credit history becoming positive and strong.

MEDITATION:

Sit quietly for a few minutes, focusing on the flame and continuing to visualize a good credit score and positive credit history.

Feel confidence and assurance in your financial stability.

CLOSING THE SPELL:

Let the candle burn completely. If you must leave it unattended, extinguish it and relight it when you can continue to focus on your intention.

Once the candle has burned out, bury any remaining wax and herbs in the earth to ground the spell and solidify your good credit.

BUSINESS SUCCESS SPELL

PURPOSE: TO ENSURE SUCCESS AND GROWTH IN YOUR BUSINESS ENDEAVORS.

MATERIALS NEEDED:

1 orange candle

Business success oil (a mix of bergamot, basil, and cedarwood essential oils)

Chamomile and cinnamon herbs

Cedarwood incense

PREPARATION:

Find a quiet and undisturbed place to perform the spell.

Gather all your materials and place them on a clean surface.

ANOINT THE CANDLE:

Hold the orange candle in your hands and close your eyes. Visualize your business thriving and achieving success.

Anoint the candle with the business success oil. Start from the middle of the candle, moving upward to the wick, and then from the middle down to the base. As you do this, focus on your intention to ensure business success.

DRESS THE CANDLE:

Roll the anointed candle in the chamomile and cinnamon herbs. These herbs are associated with success and prosperity.

SET UP THE SPACE:

Place the dressed candle in a candle holder and set it in front of you.

Light the cedarwood incense to enhance your focus and attract business success.

CASTING THE SPELL:

Light the orange candle and say the following words:

By this flame, success I see,

Business growth and prosperity.

With bergamot, basil, and cedarwood's light,

My business goals, now take flight.

So mote it be.

Visualize your business thriving, attracting customers, and achieving its goals.

MEDITATION:

Sit quietly for a few minutes, focusing on the flame and continuing to visualize success and growth in your business.

Feel confidence and determination in your business endeavors.

CLOSING THE SPELL:

Let the candle burn completely. If you must leave it unattended, extinguish it and relight it when you can continue to focus on your intention.

Once the candle has burned out, bury any remaining wax and herbs in the earth to ground the spell and make it manifest.

CLIENT ATTRACTION SPELL

PURPOSE: TO ATTRACT NEW CLIENTS AND CUSTOMERS TO YOUR BUSINESS.

MATERIALS NEEDED:

1 yellow candle

Attraction oil (a mix of lemon, orange, and cinnamon essential oils)

Sunflower petals and rosemary herbs

Lemon incense

PREPARATION:

Find a quiet and undisturbed place to perform the spell.

Gather all your materials and place them on a clean surface.

ANOINT THE CANDLE:

Hold the yellow candle in your hands and close your eyes. Visualize new clients and customers being attracted to your business.

Anoint the candle with the attraction oil. Start from the middle of the candle, moving upward to the wick, and then from the middle down to the base. As you do this, focus on your intention to attract new clients.

DRESS THE CANDLE:

Roll the anointed candle in the sunflower petals and rosemary herbs. These herbs are known for their ability to attract positive energy and success.

SET UP THE SPACE:

Place the dressed candle in a candle holder and set it in front of you.

Light the lemon incense to enhance your focus and attract clients.

CASTING THE SPELL:

Light the yellow candle and say the following words:

> *By this flame, clients I draw,*
> *New customers, without a flaw.*
> *With lemon, orange, and cinnamon's might,*
> *My business prospers, day and night.*
> *So mote it be.*

Visualize new clients and customers being drawn to your business, see your customer base growing, and feel the excitement of new business opportunities.

MEDITATION:

Sit quietly for a few minutes, focusing on the flame and continuing to visualize attracting new clients and customers.

Feel confidence and assurance in your business's ability to attract new clients.

CLOSING THE SPELL:

Let the candle burn completely. If you must leave it unattended, extinguish it and relight it when you can continue to focus on your intention.

Once the candle has burned out, bury any remaining wax and herbs in the earth to ground the spell and make it manifest.

SALES BOOST SPELL

PURPOSE: TO INCREASE SALES AND REVENUE IN YOUR BUSINESS.

MATERIALS NEEDED:

1 red candle

Sales oil (a mix of peppermint, ginger, and clove essential oils)

Cinnamon and clove herbs

Peppermint incense

PREPARATION:

Find a quiet and undisturbed place to perform the spell.

Gather all your materials and place them on a clean surface.

ANOINT THE CANDLE:

Hold the red candle in your hands and close your eyes. Visualize your sales increasing and your revenue growing.

Anoint the candle with the sales oil. Start from the middle of the candle, moving upward to the wick, and then from the middle down to the base. As you do this, focus on your intention to boost sales.

DRESS THE CANDLE:

Roll the anointed candle in the cinnamon and clove herbs. These herbs are known for their ability to attract prosperity and success.

SET UP THE SPACE:

Place the dressed candle in a candle holder and set it in front of you.

Light the peppermint incense to enhance your focus and attract sales.

CASTING THE SPELL:

Light the red candle and say the following words:

> *By this flame, sales I boost,*
> *Revenue grows, success produced.*
> *With peppermint, ginger, and clove's light,*
> *My business prospers, day and night.*
> *So mote it be.*

Visualize your sales increasing, see customers purchasing your products or services, and feel the excitement of growing revenue.

MEDITATION:

Sit quietly for a few minutes, focusing on the flame and continuing to visualize boosting sales and revenue.

Feel confidence and determination in your business's ability to increase sales.

CLOSING THE SPELL:

Let the candle burn completely. If you must leave it unattended, extinguish it and relight it when you can continue to focus on your intention.

Once the candle has burned out, bury any remaining wax and herbs in the earth to ground the spell and make it manifest.

PROFIT INCREASE SPELL

PURPOSE: TO INCREASE THE PROFITABILITY OF YOUR BUSINESS.

MATERIALS NEEDED:

1 green candle

Profit oil (a mix of basil, mint, and bergamot essential oils)

Mint and basil herbs

Bergamot incense

PREPARATION:

Find a quiet and undisturbed place to perform the spell.

Gather all your materials and place them on a clean surface.

ANOINT THE CANDLE:

Hold the green candle in your hands and close your eyes. Visualize your business's profits increasing.

Anoint the candle with the profit oil. Start from the middle of the candle, moving upward to the wick, and then from the middle down to the base. As you do this, focus on your intention to increase profits.

DRESS THE CANDLE:

Roll the anointed candle in the mint and basil herbs. These herbs are known for their ability to attract prosperity and financial success.

SET UP THE SPACE:

Place the dressed candle in a candle holder and set it in front of you.

Light the bergamot incense to enhance your focus and attract profitability.

CASTING THE SPELL:

Light the green candle and say the following words:

By this flame, profits rise,

Financial gains, my enterprise.

With basil, mint, and bergamot's might,

My business prospers, day and night.

So mote it be.

Visualize your business's profits increasing, see your revenue growing, and feel the excitement of financial success.

MEDITATION:

Sit quietly for a few minutes, focusing on the flame and continuing to visualize increasing profits.

Feel confidence and assurance in your business's ability increasing profits.

MEDITATION:

Sit quietly for a few minutes, focusing on the flame and continuing to visualize increasing profits.

Feel confidence and assurance in your business's ability to generate higher profits.

CLOSING THE SPELL:

Let the candle burn completely. If you must leave it unattended, extinguish it and relight it when you can continue to focus on your intention.

Once the candle has burned out, bury any remaining wax and herbs in the earth to ground the spell and solidify the increase in your business's profitability.

PARTNERSHIP HARMONY SPELL

PURPOSE: TO ENSURE HARMONY AND SUCCESS IN BUSINESS PARTNERSHIPS.

MATERIALS NEEDED:

1 pink candle

Harmony oil (a mix of lavender, rose, and ylang-ylang essential oils)

Rose petals and lavender herbs

Rose incense

PREPARATION:

Find a quiet and undisturbed place to perform the spell.

Gather all your materials and place them on a clean surface.

ANOINT THE CANDLE:

Hold the pink candle in your hands and close your eyes. Visualize harmony and success in your business partnerships.

Anoint the candle with the harmony oil. Start from the middle of the candle, moving upward to the wick, and then from the middle down to the base. As you do this, focus on your intention to create harmony in your business relationships.

DRESS THE CANDLE:

Roll the anointed candle in the rose petals and lavender herbs. These herbs are associated with harmony, love, and positive relationships.

SET UP THE SPACE:

Place the dressed candle in a candle holder and set it in front of you.

Light the rose incense to enhance your focus and attract harmony.

CASTING THE SPELL:

Light the pink candle and say the following words:

By this flame, harmony I call,
Partnership success for one and all.
With lavender, rose, and ylang-ylang's light,
Our business prospers, day and night.
So mote it be.

Visualize harmonious relationships with your business partners, see successful collaborations, and feel the mutual respect and understanding.

MEDITATION:

Sit quietly for a few minutes, focusing on the flame and continuing to visualize harmony and success in your business partnerships.

Feel confidence and assurance in your business relationships.

CLOSING THE SPELL:

Let the candle burn completely. If you must leave it unattended, extinguish it and relight it when you can continue to focus on your intention.

Once the candle has burned out, bury any remaining wax and herbs in the earth to ground the spell and solidify the harmony in your business partnerships.

STARTUP FUNDING SPELL

PURPOSE: TO ATTRACT FUNDING AND FINANCIAL SUPPORT FOR A NEW BUSINESS OR STARTUP.

MATERIALS NEEDED:

1 gold candle

Funding oil (a mix of bergamot, frankincense, and ginger essential oils)

Mint and bay leaf herbs

Frankincense incense

PREPARATION:

Find a quiet and undisturbed place to perform the spell.

Gather all your materials and place them on a clean surface.

ANOINT THE CANDLE:

Hold the gold candle in your hands and close your eyes. Visualize attracting funding and financial support for your new business or startup.

Anoint the candle with the funding oil. Start from the middle of the candle, moving upward to the wick, and then from the middle down to the base. As you do this, focus on your intention to attract funding.

DRESS THE CANDLE:

Roll the anointed candle in the mint and bay leaf herbs. These herbs are associated with prosperity and financial success.

SET UP THE SPACE:

Place the dressed candle in a candle holder and set it in front of you.

Light the frankincense incense to enhance your focus and attract financial support.

CASTING THE SPELL:

Light the gold candle and say the following words:

By this flame, funding I seek,
Financial support, strong and sleek.
With bergamot, frankincense, and ginger's might,
My startup prospers, day and night.
So mote it be.

Visualize financial support flowing into your business, see investors and supporters contributing to your startup, and feel the excitement of receiving funding.

MEDITATION:

Sit quietly for a few minutes, focusing on the flame and continuing to visualize attracting funding for your startup.

Feel confidence and assurance in your ability to secure financial support.

CLOSING THE SPELL:

Let the candle burn completely. If you must leave it unattended, extinguish it and relight it when you can continue to focus on your intention.

Once the candle has burned out, bury any remaining wax and herbs in the earth to ground the spell and make it manifest.

MARKET EXPANSION SPELL

PURPOSE: TO ATTRACT OPPORTUNITIES FOR BUSINESS EXPANSION INTO NEW MARKETS.

MATERIALS NEEDED:

1 purple candle

Expansion oil (a mix of clove, cinnamon, and bergamot essential oils)

Rosemary and basil herbs

Cinnamon incense

PREPARATION:

Find a quiet and undisturbed place to perform the spell.

Gather all your materials and place them on a clean surface.

ANOINT THE CANDLE:

Hold the purple candle in your hands and close your eyes. Visualize your business expanding into new markets.

Anoint the candle with the expansion oil. Start from the middle of the candle, moving upward to the wick, and then from the middle down to the base. As you do this, focus on your intention to attract market expansion opportunities.

DRESS THE CANDLE:

Roll the anointed candle in the rosemary and basil herbs. These herbs are known for their ability to attract success and new opportunities.

SET UP THE SPACE:

Place the dressed candle in a candle holder and set it in front of you.

Light the cinnamon incense to enhance your focus and attract expansion opportunities.

CASTING THE SPELL:

Light the purple candle and say the following words:

By this flame, expansion I call,

New markets open, one and all.

With clove, cinnamon, and bergamot's might,

My business grows, both day and night.

So mote it be.

Visualize your business expanding into new markets, see new opportunities arising, and feel the excitement of business growth.

MEDITATION:

Sit quietly for a few minutes, focusing on the flame and continuing to visualize attracting market expansion opportunities.

Feel confidence and assurance in your business's ability to grow and expand.

CLOSING THE SPELL:

Let the candle burn completely. If you must leave it unattended, extinguish it and relight it when you can continue to focus on your intention.

Once the candle has burned out, bury any remaining wax and herbs in the earth to ground the spell and make it manifest.

CREATIVITY SPELL

PURPOSE: TO ENHANCE INNOVATION AND CREATIVITY IN YOUR BUSINESS ENDEAVORS.

MATERIALS NEEDED:

1 orange candle

Creativity oil (a mix of orange, rosemary, and peppermint essential oils)

Orange peel and rosemary herbs

Orange incense

PREPARATION:

Find a quiet and undisturbed place to perform the spell.

Gather all your materials and place them on a clean surface.

ANOINT THE CANDLE:

Hold the orange candle in your hands and close your eyes. Visualize your business thriving with innovation and creativity.

Anoint the candle with the creativity oil. Start from the middle of the candle, moving upward to the wick, and then from the middle down to the base. As you do this, focus on your intention to enhance innovation and creativity.

DRESS THE CANDLE:

Roll the anointed candle in the orange peel and rosemary herbs. These herbs are known for their ability to stimulate creativity and innovative thinking.

SET UP THE SPACE:

Place the dressed candle in a candle holder and set it in front of you.

Light the orange incense to enhance your focus and attract creativity.

CASTING THE SPELL:

Light the orange candle and say the following words:

By this flame, creativity I spark,

Innovation grows, bright and stark.

With orange, rosemary, and peppermint's light,

My business shines, both day and night.

So mote it be.

Visualize innovative ideas flowing into your business, see creative solutions and strategies emerging, and feel the excitement of newfound creativity.

MEDITATION:

Sit quietly for a few minutes, focusing on the flame and continuing to visualize enhancing innovation and creativity in your business.

Feel confidence and assurance in your ability to generate creative ideas and solutions.

CLOSING THE SPELL:

Let the candle burn completely. If you must leave it unattended, extinguish it and relight it when you can continue to focus on your intention.

Once the candle has burned out, bury any remaining wax and herbs in the earth to ground the spell and make it manifest.

BUSINESS PROTECTION SPELL

PURPOSE: TO PROTECT YOUR BUSINESS FROM NEGATIVE INFLUENCES AND ENSURE ITS SAFETY AND SECURITY.

MATERIALS NEEDED:

1 black candle

Protection oil (a mix of eucalyptus, frankincense, and myrrh essential oils)

Bay leaf and sage herbs

Dragon's blood incense

PREPARATION:

Find a quiet and undisturbed place to perform the spell.

Gather all your materials and place them on a clean surface.

ANOINT THE CANDLE:

Hold the black candle in your hands and close your eyes. Visualize a protective barrier surrounding your business.

Anoint the candle with the protection oil. Start from the middle of the candle, moving upward to the wick, and then from the middle down to the base. As you do this, focus on your intention to protect your business.

DRESS THE CANDLE:

Roll the anointed candle in the bay leaf and sage herbs. These herbs are associated with protection and purification.

SET UP THE SPACE:

Place the dressed candle in a candle holder and set it in front of you.

Light the dragon's blood incense to enhance the protective energy of the spell.

CASTING THE SPELL:

Light the black candle and say the following words:

> By this flame, protection I seek,
> Shield my business, strong and sleek.
> With eucalyptus, frankincense, and myrrh's might,
> Guard my work both day and night.
> So mote it be.

Visualize a protective barrier surrounding your business, keeping it safe from negative influences and harm.

MEDITATION:

Sit quietly for a few minutes, focusing on the flame and continuing to visualize the protection of your business.

Feel a sense of security and assurance that your business is protected.

CLOSING THE SPELL:

Let the candle burn completely. If you must leave it unattended, extinguish it and relight it when you can continue to focus on your intention.

Once the candle has burned out, bury any remaining wax and herbs in the earth to ground the spell and solidify the protection of your business.

EMPLOYEE LOYALTY SPELL

PURPOSE: TO ENHANCE LOYALTY AND MORALE AMONG EMPLOYEES IN YOUR BUSINESS.

MATERIALS NEEDED:

1 yellow candle

Loyalty oil (a mix of lavender, rosemary, and lemon essential oils)

Rosemary and chamomile herbs

Lavender incense

PREPARATION:

Find a quiet and undisturbed place to perform the spell.

Gather all your materials and place them on a clean surface.

ANOINT THE CANDLE:

Hold the yellow candle in your hands and close your eyes. Visualize your employees feeling loyal, motivated, and happy.

Anoint the candle with the loyalty oil. Start from the middle of the candle, moving upward to the wick, and then from the middle down to the base. As you do this, focus on your intention to enhance employee loyalty.

DRESS THE CANDLE:

Roll the anointed candle in the rosemary and chamomile herbs. These herbs are known for their ability to promote loyalty and positive relationships.

SET UP THE SPACE:

Place the dressed candle in a candle holder and set it in front of you.

Light the lavender incense to enhance your focus and attract loyalty.

CASTING THE SPELL:

Light the yellow candle and say the following words:

By this flame, loyalty I call,
Employees loyal, one and all.
With lavender, rosemary, and lemon's light,
Harmony and trust, both day and night.
So mote it be.

Visualize your employees feeling loyal, motivated, and happy. See positive relationships and a harmonious work environment.

MEDITATION:

Sit quietly for a few minutes, focusing on the flame and continuing to visualize enhancing loyalty and morale among your employees.

Feel confidence and assurance in your ability to foster a positive work environment.

CLOSING THE SPELL:

Let the candle burn completely. If you must leave it unattended, extinguish it and relight it when you can continue to focus on your intention.

Once the candle has burned out, bury any remaining wax and herbs in the earth to ground the spell and make it manifest.

DEBT COLLECTION SPELL

PURPOSE: TO ASSIST IN COLLECTING OUTSTANDING DEBTS OWED TO YOU OR YOUR BUSINESS

MATERIALS NEEDED:

1 red candle

Debt collection oil (a mix of cinnamon, clove, and basil essential oils)

Bay leaf and cinnamon herbs

Clove incense

PREPARATION:

Find a quiet and undisturbed place to perform the spell.

Gather all your materials and place them on a clean surface.

ANOINT THE CANDLE:

Hold the red candle in your hands and close your eyes. Visualize the debts owed to your business being paid.

Anoint the candle with the debt collection oil. Start from the middle of the candle, moving upward to the wick, and then from the middle down to the base. As you do this, focus on your intention to collect outstanding debts.

DRESS THE CANDLE:

Roll the anointed candle in the bay leaf and cinnamon herbs. These herbs are known for their ability to attract prosperity and financial success.

SET UP THE SPACE:

Place the dressed candle in a candle holder and set it in front of you.

Light the clove incense to enhance your focus and attract debt repayment.

CASTING THE SPELL:

Light the red candle and say the following words:

> By this flame, debts be paid,
> Financial dues, no longer delayed.
> With cinnamon, clove, and basil's might,
> Collecting funds both day and night.
> So mote it be.

Visualize the debts owed to your business being paid promptly and completely.

MEDITATION:

Sit quietly for a few minutes, focusing on the flame and continuing to visualize the collection of outstanding debts.

Feel confidence and assurance in your ability to collect the debts owed to your business.

CLOSING THE SPELL:

Let the candle burn completely. If you must leave it unattended, extinguish it and relight it when you can continue to focus on your intention.

Once the candle has burned out, bury any remaining wax and herbs in the earth to ground the spell and make it manifest.

LUCKY HAND SPELL

PURPOSE: TO ENHANCE YOUR LUCK AND SUCCESS IN GAMBLING AND GAMES OF CHANCE.

MATERIALS NEEDED:

1 gold candle

Luck oil (a mix of clover, basil, and ginger essential oils)

Mint and bay leaf herbs

Cinnamon incense

PREPARATION:

Find a quiet and undisturbed place to perform the spell.

Gather all your materials and place them on a clean surface.

ANOINT THE CANDLE:

Hold the gold candle in your hands and close your eyes. Visualize yourself having a lucky hand in gambling and games of chance.

Anoint the candle with the luck oil. Start from the middle of the candle, moving upward to the wick, and then from the middle down to the base. As you do this, focus on your intention to enhance your luck.

DRESS THE CANDLE:

Roll the anointed candle in the mint and bay leaf herbs. These herbs are associated with luck and prosperity.

SET UP THE SPACE:

Place the dressed candle in a candle holder and set it in front of you.

Light the cinnamon incense to enhance your focus and attract luck.

CASTING THE SPELL:

Light the gold candle and say the following words:

> By this flame, luck I claim,
> Winning hand, in every game.
> With clover, basil, and ginger's might,
> Fortune follows both day and night.
> So mote it be.

Visualize yourself winning in gambling and games of chance, feel the excitement of your lucky streak.

MEDITATION:

Sit quietly for a few minutes, focusing on the flame and continuing to visualize enhancing your luck.

Feel confidence and assurance in your ability to attract good fortune.

CLOSING THE SPELL:

Let the candle burn completely. If you must leave it unattended, extinguish it and relight it when you can continue to focus on your intention.

Once the candle has burned out, bury any remaining wax and herbs in the earth to ground the spell and make it manifest.

WINNING STREAK SPELL

PURPOSE: TO ATTRACT A WINNING STREAK IN GAMBLING AND GAMES OF CHANCE.

MATERIALS NEEDED:

1 green candle

Winning oil (a mix of cinnamon, basil, and patchouli essential oils)

Clover and nutmeg herbs

Patchouli incense

PREPARATION:

Find a quiet and undisturbed place to perform the spell.

Gather all your materials and place them on a clean surface.

ANOINT THE CANDLE:

Hold the green candle in your hands and close your eyes. Visualize yourself on a winning streak in gambling and games of chance.

Anoint the candle with the winning oil. Start from the middle of the candle, moving upward to the wick, and then from the middle down to the base. As you do this, focus on your intention to attract a winning streak.

DRESS THE CANDLE:

Roll the anointed candle in the clover and nutmeg herbs. These herbs are known for their ability to attract luck and winning outcomes.

SET UP THE SPACE:

Place the dressed candle in a candle holder and set it in front of you.

Light the patchouli incense to enhance your focus and attract winning energy.

CASTING THE SPELL:

Light the green candle and say the following words:

> By this flame, a streak I win,
> Luck and fortune, now begin.
> With cinnamon, basil, and patchouli's might,
> Winning follows both day and night.
> So mote it be.

Visualize yourself on a winning streak in gambling and games of chance. Feel the excitement and joy of continuous wins.

MEDITATION:

Sit quietly for a few minutes, focusing on the flame and continuing to visualize a winning streak.

Feel confidence and assurance in your ability to attract winning outcomes.

CLOSING THE SPELL:

Let the candle burn completely. If you must leave it unattended, extinguish it and relight it when you can continue to focus on your intention.

Once the candle has burned out, bury any remaining wax and herbs in the earth to ground the spell and make it manifest.

SLOT MACHINE LUCK SPELL

PURPOSE: TO ATTRACT LUCK AND SUCCESS SPECIFICALLY AT SLOT MACHINES.

MATERIALS NEEDED:

1 silver candle

Slot machine luck oil (a mix of ginger, orange, and clove essential oils)

Mint and basil herbs

Ginger incense

PREPARATION:

Find a quiet and undisturbed place to perform the spell.

Gather all your materials and place them on a clean surface.

ANOINT THE CANDLE:

Hold the silver candle in your hands and close your eyes. Visualize yourself winning at slot machines.

Anoint the candle with the slot machine luck oil. Start from the middle of the candle, moving upward to the wick, and then from the middle down to the base. As you do this, focus on your intention to attract luck at slot machines.

DRESS THE CANDLE:

Roll the anointed candle in the mint and basil herbs. These herbs are known for their ability to attract luck and prosperity.

SET UP THE SPACE:

Place the dressed candle in a candle holder and set it in front of you.

Light the ginger incense to enhance your focus and attract luck.

CASTING THE SPELL:

Light the silver candle and say the following words:

> *By this flame, slot luck I seek,*
> *Winning spins, every week.*
> *With ginger, orange, and clove's might,*
> *Slot machine fortune, day and night.*
> *So mote it be.*

Visualize yourself winning at slot machines, feel the excitement of hitting jackpots and big wins.

MEDITATION:

Sit quietly for a few minutes, focusing on the flame and continuing to visualize winning at slot machines.

Feel confidence and assurance in your ability to attract good fortune at slots.

CLOSING THE SPELL:

Let the candle burn completely. If you must leave it unattended, extinguish it and relight it when you can continue to focus on your intention.

Once the candle has burned out, bury any remaining wax and herbs in the earth to ground the spell and make it manifest.

POKER FORTUNE SPELL

PURPOSE: TO ATTRACT LUCK AND SUCCESS SPECIFICALLY IN POKER GAMES.

MATERIALS NEEDED:

1 red candle

Poker luck oil (a mix of cinnamon, nutmeg, and patchouli essential oils)

Basil and clover herbs

Cinnamon incense

PREPARATION:

Find a quiet and undisturbed place to perform the spell.

Gather all your materials and place them on a clean surface.

ANOINT THE CANDLE:

Hold the red candle in your hands and close your eyes. Visualize yourself winning in poker games.

Anoint the candle with the poker luck oil. Start from the middle of the candle, moving upward to the wick, and then from the middle down to the base. As you do this, focus on your intention to attract luck in poker.

DRESS THE CANDLE:

Roll the anointed candle in the basil and clover herbs. These herbs are associated with luck and prosperity.

SET UP THE SPACE:

Place the dressed candle in a candle holder and set it in front of you.

Light the cinnamon incense to enhance your focus and attract luck.

CASTING THE SPELL:

Light the red candle and say the following words:

> By this flame, poker luck I claim,
> Winning hands, fortune's game.
> With cinnamon, nutmeg, and patchouli's might,
> Poker success, both day and night.
> So mote it be.

Visualize yourself winning in poker games, see yourself making successful bets and strategic moves.

MEDITATION:

Sit quietly for a few minutes, focusing on the flame and continuing to visualize winning in poker games.

Feel confidence and assurance in your ability to attract good fortune in poker.

CLOSING THE SPELL:

Let the candle burn completely. If you must leave it unattended, extinguish it and relight it when you can continue to focus on your intention.

Once the candle has burned out, bury any remaining wax and herbs in the earth to ground the spell and make it manifest.

ROULETTE SUCCESS SPELL

PURPOSE: TO ATTRACT LUCK AND SUCCESS SPECIFICALLY IN ROULETTE GAMES.

MATERIALS NEEDED:

1 green candle

Roulette luck oil (a mix of basil, ginger, and clove essential oils)

Bay leaf and cinnamon herbs

Ginger incense

PREPARATION:

Find a quiet and undisturbed place to perform the spell.

Gather all your materials and place them on a clean surface.

ANOINT THE CANDLE:

Hold the green candle in your hands and close your eyes. Visualize yourself winning in roulette games.

Anoint the candle with the roulette luck oil. Start from the middle of the candle, moving upward to the wick, and then from the middle down to the base. As you do this, focus on your intention to attract luck in roulette.

DRESS THE CANDLE:

Roll the anointed candle in the bay leaf and cinnamon herbs. These herbs are known for their ability to attract luck and prosperity.

SET UP THE SPACE:

Place the dressed candle in a candle holder and set it in front of you.

Light the ginger incense to enhance your focus and attract luck.

CASTING THE SPELL:

Light the green candle and say the following words:

By this flame, roulette luck I seek,

Winning spins, strong and sleek.

With basil, ginger, and clove's might,

Roulette success, both day and night.

So mote it be.

Visualize yourself winning in roulette games, feel the excitement of hitting winning numbers.

MEDITATION:

Sit quietly for a few minutes, focusing on the flame and continuing to visualize winning in roulette games.

Feel confidence and assurance in your ability to attract good fortune in roulette.

CLOSING THE SPELL:

Let the candle burn completely. If you must leave it unattended, extinguish it and relight it when you can continue to focus on your intention.

Once the candle has burned out, bury any remaining wax and herbs in the earth to ground the spell and make it manifest.

LOTTERY WINNING SPELL

PURPOSE: TO ATTRACT LUCK AND SUCCESS IN LOTTERY GAMES.

MATERIALS NEEDED:

1 gold candle

Lottery luck oil (a mix of clover, basil, and orange essential oils)

Bay leaf and mint herbs

Basil incense

PREPARATION:

Find a quiet and undisturbed place to perform the spell.

Gather all your materials and place them on a clean surface.

ANOINT THE CANDLE:

Hold the gold candle in your hands and close your eyes. Visualize yourself winning the lottery.

Anoint the candle with the lottery luck oil. Start from the middle of the candle, moving upward to the wick, and then from the middle down to the base. As you do this, focus on your intention to attract luck in the lottery.

DRESS THE CANDLE:

Roll the anointed candle in the bay leaf and mint herbs. These herbs are associated with luck and prosperity.

SET UP THE SPACE:

Place the dressed candle in a candle holder and set it in front of you.

Light the basil incense to enhance your focus and attract luck.

CASTING THE SPELL:

Light the gold candle and say the following words:

> By this flame, lottery luck I call,
> Winning numbers, now befall.
> With clover, basil, and orange's might,
> Lottery success, both day and night.
> So mote it be.

Visualize yourself winning the lottery, see yourself holding a winning ticket, and feel the excitement of the win.

MEDITATION:

Sit quietly for a few minutes, focusing on the flame and continuing to visualize winning the lottery.

MEDITATION:

Sit quietly for a few minutes, focusing on the flame and continuing to visualize winning the lottery.

Feel confidence and assurance in your ability to attract good fortune in lottery games.

CLOSING THE SPELL:

Let the candle burn completely. If you must leave it unattended, extinguish it and relight it when you can continue to focus on your intention.

Once the candle has burned out, bury any remaining wax and herbs in the earth to ground the spell and make it manifest.

BETTING WISDOM SPELL

PURPOSE: TO ENHANCE YOUR WISDOM AND DECISION-MAKING SKILLS IN BETTING AND GAMBLING.

MATERIALS NEEDED:

1 purple candle

Wisdom oil (a mix of sage, frankincense, and sandalwood essential oils)

Sage and rosemary herbs

Sage incense

PREPARATION:

Find a quiet and undisturbed place to perform the spell.

Gather all your materials and place them on a clean surface.

ANOINT THE CANDLE:

Hold the purple candle in your hands and close your eyes. Visualize yourself making wise and successful betting decisions.

Anoint the candle with the wisdom oil. Start from the middle of the candle, moving upward to the wick, and then from the middle down to the base. As you do this, focus on your intention to enhance your betting wisdom.

DRESS THE CANDLE:

Roll the anointed candle in the sage and rosemary herbs. These herbs are associated with wisdom and clarity.

SET UP THE SPACE:

Place the dressed candle in a candle holder and set it in front of you.

Light the sage incense to enhance your focus and attract wisdom.

CASTING THE SPELL:

Light the purple candle and say the following words:

By this flame, wisdom I seek,

Betting decisions, strong and sleek.

With sage, frankincense, and sandalwood's might,

Wisdom guides me, both day and night.

So mote it be.

Visualize yourself making wise and successful betting decisions, see yourself analyzing bets with clarity and insight.

MEDITATION:

Sit quietly for a few minutes, focusing on the flame and continuing to visualize enhancing your betting wisdom.

Feel confidence and assurance in your ability to make wise betting decisions.

CLOSING THE SPELL:

Let the candle burn completely. If you must leave it unattended, extinguish it and relight it when you can continue to focus on your intention.

Once the candle has burned out, bury any remaining wax and herbs in the earth to ground the spell and make it manifest.

SAFE GAMBLING SPELL
TO ENSURE SAFE AND RESPONSIBLE GAMBLING PRACTICES.

MATERIALS NEEDED:

1 white candle

Safety oil (a mix of lavender, eucalyptus, and chamomile essential oils)

Chamomile and rosemary herbs

Lavender incense

PREPARATION:

Find a quiet and undisturbed place to perform the spell.

Gather all your materials and place them on a clean surface.

ANOINT THE CANDLE:

Hold the white candle in your hands and close your eyes. Visualize yourself engaging in safe and responsible gambling practices.

Anoint the candle with the safety oil. Start from the middle of the candle, moving upward to the wick, and then from the middle down to the base. As you do this, focus on your intention to ensure safe gambling.

DRESS THE CANDLE:

Roll the anointed candle in the chamomile and rosemary herbs. These herbs are associated with safety and clarity.

SET UP THE SPACE:

Place the dressed candle in a candle holder and set it in front of you.

Light the lavender incense to enhance your focus and attract safety.

CASTING THE SPELL:

Light the white candle and say the following words:

> *By this flame, safety I call,*
>
> *Gambling wisely, not to fall.*
>
> *With lavender, eucalyptus, and chamomile's might,*
>
> *Safe practices, both day and night.*
>
> *So mote it be.*

Visualize yourself gambling responsibly, setting limits, and staying in control.

MEDITATION:

Sit quietly for a few minutes, focusing on the flame and continuing to visualize safe and responsible gambling practices.

Feel confidence and assurance in your ability to gamble responsibly.

CLOSING THE SPELL:

Let the candle burn completely. If you must leave it unattended, extinguish it and relight it when you can continue to focus on your intention.

Once the candle has burned out, bury any remaining wax and herbs in the earth to ground the spell and make it manifest.

JACKPOT ATTRACTION SPELL

PURPOSE: TO ATTRACT WINNING JACKPOTS IN GAMBLING AND GAMES OF CHANCE.

MATERIALS NEEDED:

1 gold candle

Jackpot oil (a mix of cinnamon, clove, and orange essential oils)

Mint and bay leaf herbs

Cinnamon incense

PREPARATION:

Find a quiet and undisturbed place to perform the spell.

Gather all your materials and place them on a clean surface.

ANOINT THE CANDLE:

Hold the gold candle in your hands and close your eyes. Visualize yourself winning jackpots in gambling and games of chance.

Anoint the candle with the jackpot oil. Start from the middle of the candle, moving upward to the wick, and then from the middle down to the base. As you do this, focus on your intention to attract winning jackpots.

DRESS THE CANDLE:

Roll the anointed candle in the mint and bay leaf herbs. These herbs are associated with luck and prosperity.

SET UP THE SPACE:

Place the dressed candle in a candle holder and set it in front of you.

Light the cinnamon incense to enhance your focus and attract jackpots.

CASTING THE SPELL:

Light the gold candle and say the following words:

By this flame, jackpots I call,

Winning big, once and for all.

With cinnamon, clove, and orange's might,

Jackpot success, both day and night.

So mote it be.

Visualize yourself winning jackpots, feel the excitement of hitting big wins and major prizes.

MEDITATION:

Sit quietly for a few minutes, focusing on the flame and continuing to visualize winning jackpots.

Feel confidence and assurance in your ability to attract winning jackpots.

CLOSING THE SPELL:

Let the candle burn completely. If you must leave it unattended, extinguish it and relight it when you can continue to focus on your intention.

Once the candle has burned out, bury any remaining wax and herbs in the earth to ground the spell and make it manifest.

BLESSINGS AND FAREWELL

Dear Reader,

As you close this book, may you carry with you the wisdom and power to transform your financial reality. The spells and blessings within these pages are not just words, but tools for creating a life of abundance, security, and joy.

Remember, the magic within you is limitless. Use it with intention, gratitude, and respect. May your path be illuminated with prosperity, and may your heart be light with the assurance that you are always guided and supported by the universe.

Thank you for embarking on this journey with "Money Spells." May your financial dreams come true, and may you inspire others with your success.

Blessed be, and may fortune favor you always.

With light and love, I leave your these special blessings for you:

FINANCIAL ABUNDANCE BLESSING

May your days be filled with prosperity and your nights with peace.

May the flow of wealth and abundance come to you with ease.

With each step you take, may success follow close behind,

And may your heart and mind be open to the riches you find.

PROTECTION BLESSING

May a shield of protection surround your financial endeavors,

Guarding against harm and ensuring your success forever.

May your wealth be safe, your fortune secure,

And may your financial journey be steady and sure.

GRATITUDE BLESSING

May you always find reasons to be thankful each day,

For the blessings you receive and the challenges you face along the way.

May gratitude open doors to even greater wealth,

And may you enjoy prosperity with joy and good health.

Victoria Rey

© All rights reserved. No part of this book may be reproduced in text or images by any means, without written permission.

© Calli Casa Editorial 2013
© Yhacar Trust, 2024

General Supervision: Bernabé Pérez.
www.2GoodLuck.com
Calli Casa Editorial
Lake Elsinore, CA 92530

www.ingramcontent.com/pod-product-compliance
Lightning Source LLC
Chambersburg PA
CBHW060854050426
42453CB00008B/976